How to be cool

Written by Sandy McKay

raintree
a Capstone company — publishers for children

The sun is a mass of burning gas.

We need the sun. It is light for us to see by.

It turns seeds into food to keep us fed.

But the sun is hot and it cannot be turned off. So, if living things are too hot, they have to cool down.

There are lots of things they do to be cooler.

Shed fur or hair

'Shedding' is 'getting rid of' hair or fur. A light coat of fur is better than a thick one if the sun is hot. So, a lot of shedding happens in the summer.

Cats and dogs shed fur.

This one sheds, too. Can you see the hair in the air?

Look at this fur being shed.

Get out of the sun!

Dark or wet corners are good if the sun is out.
A fox can go into his dim den.
A hen can sit in her coop – cooling her chicks under her wing.

A toad can go in the wet reeds.

A lizard might sit under a rock if it is too hot. If it gets too cool, it hops back out into the sun.

Hug the bark

Look at this one hugging the bark. He has thick fur so it is hard to get cool if the sun is hot. This bark is cooler than the air. So, hugging the bark cools him down a bit.

Have a dip in a pool

A dip is good if it is hot. A pet cat will not do it, but a big cat might.

Have a dip in mud

Mud can be cooling. Cows will sit in mud to cool down. The mud gets rid of bugs on them, as well.

This one will go in mud, too. It keeps cool, but it looks a mess.

This one is a fan of mud, as well.

Wag ears

If you have big, thin ears, you can wag or 'fan' them to cool down. Wagging your ears fans cool air on you.

Fan wings

Wings can keep you cool if you have them.

A bee can fan its wings to keep the air cool.

If it is too hot, a moth will fan its wings, too.

Nap for weeks . . .

It is good to have a nap if it gets too hot. But a nap might not be a short nap in the morning or the night. The nap might be for weeks and weeks until it is not so hot. It might be for **all** of the long, hot summer!

We have long, *long* naps.

And we all do, too.

. . . or nap for years!

If the sun is so hot that the river is no longer wet, a lungfish might dig into the mud on the river bed. And it will have a long, long, **long** nap there. A lungfish can nap for up to 3 years!

Pop up a parasol

This one has a big fur tail. Its tail keeps the sun off its back. Its tail is a parasol to keep it cool!

Odd tips for chilling out

A kangaroo licks its arms to cool down.

Kangaroos have naps in the hot sun. They wait to feed in the cooler night.

If it is too hot, a bat will lick its wings to keep cool. It can fan them, too. And bats might nap in cool roofs on a hot summer night.

Dogs puff if they get too hot. Short puffs get rid of the hot air in them. This cools dogs down.

Have you seen a dog do this?

Cats do this, too. An owl can do this sort of thing, as well.

This one has long legs. Long legs keep it up and off the hot soil, so it keeps cooler.

If you have long legs, a long neck is needed, too!

This dog digs a big den in the soil. It digs lots of gaps down to the den, so that the air in the den will be cooler.

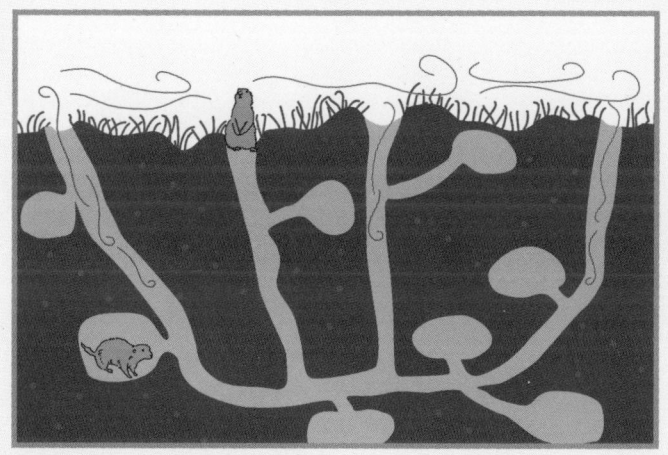

If a fish is too hot, it might dash deep into the river. It is cooler down there.

How to be cool – tips for you

If the sun is hot, there are things that you can do to be cool, too.
You can …
picnic by a river,
chill out in a pool,
turn on a fan,
soak your feet in a bucket,
sit in a sink (if you fit) and turn on the tap,
pop on a hat,
button up your top to keep the sun off,
or hang out in a hammock.